How to Avoid Drama, Defiance, and Danger as a Modern Day Parent of Teenagers

Mason Duchatschek
Sean Mulroney
Tina Meier

© 2016 by Mason Duchatschek, Sean Mulroney, Tina Meier

All rights reserved.

Trust and Verify: How to Avoid Drama, Defiance, and Danger as a Modern Day Parent of Teenagers

Table of Contents

Chapter 1:
The Bond of Trust

Ben Franklin once said, "Wise is the man who fixes his roof before it rains." If ole Ben were alive today, I'm certain he would encourage parents to sit down with their kids long before common problems were likely to occur to lay out their expectations, the tools at their disposal, and the rewards and consequences tied to the choices their kids made.

Kids need to know that their parents are on their side and that they are united against common foes and risky behaviors. Parents need to let their teens know they are providing them with a "socially acceptable" excuse to deter pushy peers from convincing them to make bad decisions. What could be a more potent response for teens than "I can't because my parents are checking"?

Ronald Reagan, in dealing with the Soviet Union during the Cold War, took a "trust and verify" approach that when applied by parents properly in this capacity can help parents and teens find a reasonable middle ground. Trust without verification removes the leverage and power the bond of trust has on teens. Many teens believe (and rightfully so) that their parents are easily duped and don't know what's going on. With this belief, teens doubt their mischief will ever be discovered and don't feel their parental bond of trust is in jeopardy. Little or no behavioral deterrent exists. Additionally, without verification, a window of opportunity exists for uninformed parents to cause damage to the bond of trust by falsely assuming that their kids aren't deserving of their trust and treating them accordingly.

Sexual predators targeting children in Internet chat rooms, temptations to drive recklessly and at high speeds, and substance abuse all threaten the lives and well-being of teens.

Most parents, whether they know it, or will admit it, have teens who have been at risk from these dangers.

And in some situations, it's not unreasonable for critics of a "trust and verify" parenting style to argue that kids should be given room to make their own choices and learn from their own mistakes. However, we believe that common sense dictates, when context is taken into consideration, that consequences of some bad choices are so severe that they don't fall in the category of "child's play." When it comes to risky behaviors like heroin, cocaine, or meth use, driving at 100+ mph, interacting with sexual predators and such, parental involvement and oversight are recommended.

Where should parents draw the line in their family's personal battle with the people and activities that put a teen's life and well-being at stake? Are parents even in the fight? How committed are they and for how long?

The enemy is present and totally committed. Parents are woefully outnumbered and surrounded, and their enemy will never, ever give up. However, in parents' arsenal, they possess the most powerful weapon of all. If misused, this weapon could be ineffective and may even backfire. What is this weapon? It's the bond of trust between parents and their teens.

If decisions are only as sound as the facts on which they are based, more information is better than less. Facts trump gut instinct, and it's better to get important information sooner rather than later. Parents have access to the most powerful weapons in the battle. It's simply up to them to use them wisely.

Why would parents object to putting a GPS system in their teen's car to alert them when their teens broke family rules (and often laws) by driving their car too far, too fast, or recklessly? Why would they scoff at the idea of putting software capable of retrieving their teen's email and Internet chat room discussions on their family computer? Knowing that substance abuse is illegal, addictive, and deadly, why would parents refuse to implement a home drug testing program that would allow them to know which, if any, substances their teens were using? While parents as well as teens value the bond of trust, some choose to believe that merely suggesting that these tools may be necessary makes them the first to break that bond.

Consequently, advances in technology that make these accurate, real-time tools available to parents often go unused until it's too late. Often, parents unwilling to use such tools, or use them properly, will accept heavier losses if not outright defeat. Quality intelligence gathering is the cornerstone of an effective battle plan.

"Pride goeth before destruction, and an haughty spirit before a fall." - Proverbs 16:18

Nobody's perfect. That includes me, you, and your children. Unfortunately, some imperfections are more dangerous to us, our families, and our children than others.

When it comes to parenting, pride and naivety are two of the most damaging.

I cringe every time I hear parents say things like:

"That would never happen to _____." (As if it couldn't.)

"My kid would never _____." (As if he/she wouldn't.)

"I already talked to my kid about _____." (As if that were enough.)

Why do pride and naivety bother me so much? It has been my experience that love is blind, and far too many people only see the best in themselves and their children. I don't fault them. Nor do I blame them. Who doesn't want to see the best in their children? We all do and that's OK as long as we don't fail to recognize and avoid the most dangerous perils and pitfalls as well.

God could have made children completely self-sufficient when they left the womb, but he didn't. Kids need parental guidance. They need direction and assistance from those of us who have already traveled the road of adolescence.

If you hiked through the Swiss Alps, it would be far easier, less dangerous, and more fulfilling to have an experienced guide lead you. He would show you features that you would normally miss, and he would warn you about difficult parts of your journey. Just as your kids rely on you to be their guide, we wrote this book so other parents can be your guide.

Our goal isn't to tell you how to do your job as parents. Our goal is to provide you with options, perspectives, and valuable experiences that complement and enhance what you're already doing.

When you consider that the teen years are a period of intense growth, not only physically but morally and intellectually, it's understandable that it's a time of confusion and upheaval for many families. Despite some adults' negative perceptions about teens, they are often energetic, thoughtful, and idealistic, with a deep interest in what's fair and right. So, although it can be a period marked by conflict between parents and their children, the teen years are also a time where significant physical, intellectual, and emotional growth transforms them greatly. Being transformed into "what" is where you come in.

Many kids announce the onset of adolescence with dramatic changes in behavior around their parents. They're starting to separate from Mom and Dad and to demonstrate more independence. At the same time, they become increasingly aware of how others, especially their peers, see them and desperately try to fit in.

Kids often start "trying on" different looks and identities. They become very aware of how they differ from their peers. The approval of their peers often becomes more important than that of their parents when it comes to making decisions.

As teens mature, they start to think more abstractly and rationally. They're forming their moral code. And parents often find that kids who previously had been willing to conform to please them suddenly begin asserting themselves—and their opinions—strongly and rebelling against parental guidance. You should expect some mood changes in your typically sunny child, and be prepared for more conflict as he or she matures as an individual.

Be prepared and remain alert. Detective Jason Grellner, with the Franklin County Narcotics Unit (Missouri) advises parents that if they ever hear their teen come home and say something like, "Mom, you won't believe what my friend _____ did. He/she did_____," to think twice before they respond. Why? Because, according to Grellner, the chances are good that their teen did the same thing and just wants to see how their parents will respond, so they know what to expect if/when their parents find out they did it, too.

Parents who know what's coming can cope with it better. And the more you know, the better you can prepare. Our kids may not be 100% of our population, but they are 100% of our future, so it is important that as many of us as possible do a good job of parenting them.

From the time kids are little they are taught to "just say no" to drugs and other risky and/or dangerous activities. The problem is that they often don't know what to say or do next, when the peer pressure doesn't go away and often gets worse.

"Peer Pressure"

When some teens do say no to drugs and other risky behaviors, their "friends" often pile on more pressure. It gets worse. The "friends" claim it's cool, it's fun, and that your "square" kid needs to loosen up and have a little fun because your kid(s) don't know what they're missing.

"C'mon man, nobody is going to know." "I've tried it myself and it hasn't hurt me." "Don't be such a sissy!" "We won't get caught." "You don't know what you're missing!"

"Good Kids Do Dumb Things"

Some of you might be thinking that your kid or your kid's friends are "good kids" and they would never try drugs, engage in risky behaviors, or hang out with other kids who do. Think again.

Here's the problem: "Good kids" do dumb things, make poor choices and mistakes, too. They aren't immune from peer pressure. Curiosity affects them, too. It's part of being a kid.

"My Kids Wouldn't Lie to Me"

I hate to break it to you, but yes they will. Kids have been telling lies to parents to stay out of trouble since the beginning of time. Here's why: If kids value the bond of trust they have with their parents and don't want to disappoint them or lose the freedoms and privileges they've "earned" by staying out of trouble, many will lie to keep from jeopardizing it.

When I hear parents tell me their kid "looked them in the eye" and said they "didn't do anything wrong" (despite hard evidence otherwise), I can only shake my head when the parent falls for it. Don't be that gullible.

"Rose-Colored Glasses"

"Good kids" who want to use and/or experiment with drugs and other dangerous activities know how to leverage the fact they haven't been in trouble (yet) or been caught. They know their actions receive less scrutiny because their parents don't think "their kid" would ever be involved in those things. And lots of teens are correct, and lots of parents are naive.

Life is about choices. It always has been. If you make good choices, you get rewards. If you make poor choices, there are consequences. Kids need to know this. Parents need to tell their kids, and parents need to point it out early and often in their kids' lives.

Tom Peters, best-selling author and management consultant, has often been credited with the old management adage "What gets measured, gets done." W. Edwards Deming has often been credited with one similar that says "You can expect what you inspect." As a parent, you are the CEO of your household, and the advice from Peters and Deming apply to you and your relationship with your kids, too.

Would your kids clean their room, take out the trash, and make their bed every time you asked if they knew you would never check? Would kids study as hard in school as they do now if their teachers never gave tests or their parents never checked their report cards? Of course not.

Chapter Two:
Parenting Tools

Up-Front Conversations or "Stealth Mode"

GPS

When I was 16, I was in the National Honor Society, made good grades, and was a varsity letterman in both cross-country and track. By anyone's definition, I was responsible. I had part-time jobs and never did drugs, ever. My "risky" behavior of choice was irresponsible and fast (really fast) driving.

I owned a silver 1976 Datsun 280Z sports car. I loved to drive fast, really fast (over 120 mph), and I did it often.

My parents did their job: I was adequately warned of the dangers of driving fast. A lack of education or the intelligence necessary to understand the warnings I was given were not the problem. I knew that if I got a speeding ticket, my driving privileges would be suspended. I knew that if I crashed my car at a high rate of speed, it could kill me or leave me with physical and/or mental disabilities.

Education and clear communication related to the rewards (i.e., continued driving privileges) and consequences (revoked driving privileges) of my behavior was a good start, but it wasn't enough to keep me from driving fast.

Why? Because I thought that as long as I was careful and didn't get caught driving fast, I wouldn't violate the bond of trust I had with my parents and I wouldn't lose my driving privileges. What my parents told me was "Don't drive fast," but my teenage brain interpreted it as "you won't get in trouble if you don't get caught."

Fortunately, I never crashed my car at high speeds, nor injured myself or anyone else. In attempts to "be responsible," I would find straight, rarely traveled roads way outside of town, and I would drive them back and forth a few times to make sure there were no speed traps. Once I knew it was clear and there were no other cars coming, I would hit the gas. I never got any tickets driving my car over 100 mph, either.

So, what would have worked? I will tell you. If my parents would have had access to GPS tracking (which exists now and is very reasonably priced), then they could have not only had a conversation about the dangers and consequences of driving irresponsibly, but they could have added the one thing that would have changed my behavior: accountability.

Replacing the "possibility" of my parents catching me (and having my driving privileges revoked or suspended) with the "absolute certainty" of my parents catching me would have done it. My choices and actions (being careful not to get caught) reduced the "possibility" of being caught enough that I felt the minimal risk was worth the fun and excitement of driving fast.

Reasonably priced GPS technology allows parents the ability to know if their teen driver exceeds a speed limit, goes outside of a mutually-agreed mileage radius and can track a vehicle at all times to know where it is, where it has been, and for how long.

Some parents opt to put a GPS system on their teen's car without telling them. That way they know if or when their teen is breaking their rules and if their son or daughter is telling the truth when asked about driving too fast or going somewhere he or she isn't supposed to be.

I happen to believe that plenty of kids (yes, even yours or mine) would lie by omission, tell partial truths, or even tell outright whoppers to protect the bond of trust they have with their parents if they don't think they've done anything to get caught, can get their friends to back them up and lie for them, or think their story will stick.

If your choice is to use technology in "stealth mode" (without telling them), are you prepared to explain to your kids how you know they lied to you after the fact? Or, will you feel compelled to tell a lie to keep your secret (e.g., a friend of ours saw your car, you passed someone we know on

Main Street at a high rate of speed and they called us, etc.)? If you choose the latter, if (or when) your son or daughter ever finds out the truth, it will be awfully difficult to explain the virtues of honesty to your kids having been dishonest yourself....

The other option (and the one I prefer) is to communicate the dangers, rules, and responsibilities of automobile safety up front. It shouldn't be that hard to explain to your son or daughter that you care for their safety and if they are ever in trouble, you want to know ASAP so you can help. If they are ever driving to places they shouldn't be or in ways that are dangerous to them or others, you want to know that ASAP also. If they experience peer pressure to go fast or someplace they shouldn't, then you've given them a "socially acceptable" and "built-in" excuse not to.

Breathalyzer

Want to keep your teen from driving under the influence, especially if they "feel OK" to drive? Want to make sure your teen doesn't ride with someone else who is under the influence of alcohol but "feels OK" to drive?

There are all kinds of options available for purchase ranging anywhere from $15–$150 in price. If your teen offers a friend willing to drive access to their test "just to make sure" their friend doesn't get in an accident or get a DWI on their record, they come off as being a good friend and may save a life including their own. If it means the driver waits long enough to sober up, instead of hopping in a car and driving off, then hindsight will prove the investment was worth it.

Keylogger Software

You can't know about everything your kids are doing online. Or can you?

Some parents not only explain the dangers associated with Internet usage, they also put in strict rules to prohibit the use of some sites, require their teens to share all their passwords and usernames for any sites (especially social media sites) they use, and/or use a computer in a common area of the house. Some parents even log in once in a while as their teen to check on the nature of conversations and the other participants (friends) involved in their teen's life.

Software known as "keylogger software" exists that parents can purchase for well under $100, even under $30, that gives them the power to:

- Filter and block inappropriate online content

- Block chat and instant messenger conversations

- Prevent file transfers (FTP, peer to peer, USB drives, etc.)

- Block usage of social networking sites

- Prevent the display of undesirable, inappropriate, or questionable search results

- Block loading and usage of specific applications or programs

- Prevent access to online games based on ratings (E-everyone, M-mature, etc.)

- Disguise inappropriate language in content allowed on other sites (comments, etc.)

The software options that exist also allow for recording of things like online searches, websites that are visited, emails that are sent, posts made on social media accounts, usernames and passwords, and chat room discussions. The software also offers options like remote management and scheduled monitoring (so you can select specific dates and/or times for monitoring). It works on Android, iPhone, Mac, and IBM-compatible PC's.

So the big question remaining is do you establish the rules of Internet access and let your teen know that you are checking and how you are doing it, or do you do it in "stealth mode" without him or her knowing it? That's your call, and the best answer depends on your teen and your situation.

Keylogger software may be good when children are younger such as elementary and middle school age, but the hope is that by the time they get to high school you don't have such strict measures. If there are parents that have children that continuously make bad decisions when it comes to the Internet or children that may be more vulnerable, this may make more sense for them.

Like any other tool, these are worthless if you don't actually follow through and check what you promise you will check.

Drug Detection and Prevention

Teens typically fall into one of three categories when it comes to substance use:

1. Non-users

2. Experimenters

3. Committed/Habitual/Addicted Users

If your teen is a non-user, your goal is to keep them that way. If your teen has experimented, does experiment, or is willing to experiment, your goal is to prevent their assimilation into a dependency on the chemicals and the culture of trouble it attracts.

Again, your ability to make good parenting decisions is only as sound as the facts on which they are based. Can you handle the truth? Of course you can.

When it comes to drug use, how can you get the facts you need? How can you influence your teen to make good choices when he or she gets the peer pressure to make bad choices?

Let's start by talking about kids and their challenges:

If you don't think your kid would ever use drugs because your kid is a choirboy, is in the drama club, or is a star athlete, then I would ask you to consider this: How many musicians do you know of who have had drug issues? How many actors or actresses do you know of who have had drug problems? How many stories do you need to hear about college or professional athletes who ended up losing it all because of drugs?

First, kids have all been taught to "just say no." Unfortunately, nobody ever told them what to say next, and the pressure doesn't stop there and often gets worse. That's when their buddies start piling on with "Oh, don't be such a sissy or wimp. Nobody's gonna find out. What's the big deal?" You know how it goes.

It's been my experience that kids need a socially acceptable excuse and the words "No thanks. My parents test me." stop pushy peers in their tracks. It's the socially acceptable excuse kids need to sidestep peer pressure without feeling awkward in front of their supposed friends.

Second, kids value the bond of trust they have with their parents, and as long as they don't think they'll get caught doing something wrong, then they don't feel their bond of trust is ever in jeopardy and a bunch of them will simply do whatever they want. If there's no harm, there's no foul. However, if they know they will get caught and ruin a bond of trust with their parents and face stiff consequences, then the temptation to give drugs a try isn't so appealing.

Let's talk about parents and their challenges.

When parents talk to their kids about drugs, it's a good start. But if explaining the dangers of irresponsible choices was enough, then we wouldn't need police sobriety checkpoints or speeding tickets, because everyone knows it's dangerous to drive drunk and/or drive fast.

Some drink and drive anyway and hope they don't get caught. I suspect fewer would make those same choices if they knew for sure that they'd get caught.

Consider implementing a properly administered home drug test program. Let me define in specific terms what that means and then describe the steps.

Step 1: As a parent, it's important to talk to your kid in advance of any issues and explain that life is about choices. If you make good choices in life, you get rewards. If you make bad choices in life, you have to face the consequences.

Step 2: As a parent, you should explain that you know drugs are an issue in your community, that peers do or will apply pressure, and you want to give them a way out. You don't care if their friends think you are cool. You know the pressure can be intense and you want to reward them for having the character and strength to say no. Let them know you're going to start testing randomly using a computer program that selects random dates. Let them know you also reserve the right to hit them up with an unannounced test if they act differently than normal or you suspect usage at any time.

Tell them you want to celebrate drug-free results like A's on a report card and let them pick out a CD, DVD, or video game of their choice each time they pass the test. It's very important to catch kids doing the right things and celebrate it often.

You also need to tell your kids that if they make poor choices and test positive then very specific consequences will exist. Let them know that they can say goodbye to their car keys, video game system, cellphone and other privileges for awhile. They can earn their privileges back along with your trust as they pass more frequent follow-up tests.

Without that kind of follow-up plan, parents and the teens they've caught using often struggle to repair their broken bond of trust. An arrangement like this provides a simple pathway to repairing that damaged relationship sooner rather than later.

Home drug test kits (see http://www.testmyteen.com) work like home pregnancy kits, except they detect recent drug use. There are many options, some of which offer you lab quality accuracy in a matter of minutes without having to send any samples to a lab. In most cases, you don't have to be a doctor or technician to read the results, and since there are no labs or doctors involved, there is no record of results anywhere. The truth is shared between you and your son or daughter.

Types of Popular Tests

1. Saliva-based drug tests are meant to detect recent drug usage. They sound great in theory because no urine collection is necessary and they can be administered almost anywhere. Unfortunately, the window of detection for drugs like marijuana is so short (a matter of hours after usage) that their effectiveness and accuracy leave something to be desired and I don't recommend these for home use.

2. By far, the most popular tests for recent drug usage (for good reason) are urine-based tests. The best kits have clear cup designs (so it is easy to see if foreign substances have been added to adulterate or tamper with results). They also have temperature strips so you know it is a fresh warm sample and not a "clean substitute" from a drug-free friend that has been hidden in your house or bathroom for such an occasion, or one that has been dipped in water to dilute the sample you collected. The best kits also have adulterant detectors built in to help identify attempts to add foreign substances (typically purchased on the Internet to help people try to "beat" a drug test). Depending on a person's metabolism, body composition, hydration levels, frequency, and the duration of drug usage, urine-based kits can detect recent drug usage for most drugs for a week to ten days past the last usage. For heavy marijuana users who have been using for years, the urine kits may show positive results for as long as twenty-one to thirty days.

3. Hair-based tests do require that a sample of hair be taken at home and sent to a lab. Usually, you are given a phone number or website you can contact along with a code to get your results. Hair tests are significantly more expensive, incredibly

accurate, and reveal a drug use history going back ninety days.

These tests make it possible to detect the use of the most popular street drugs as well as prescriptions that are also commonly abused (marijuana, cocaine, methamphetamines, ecstasy, opiates, amphetamines, methadone, oxycodone, etc.).

Prescription Drug Temptation

If you don't think your children would purchase street drugs, you might (or might not) be right. But don't be surprised if they are raiding the medicine cabinets of your family members and friends. They often do so with a false sense of safety and security. It is remarkable how many kids think it's safe to use prescription drugs because they don't have to risk arrest like they would if they bought from a drug dealer and/or "it must be safe" because a doctor prescribed them.

Avoiding Conflict over Results

When positive results appear, some kids will claim that the kits are defective. Others will claim that they were "the only ones" in a room full of people using drugs that didn't do it, too, and that "secondhand smoke" was the reason for the positive results. (They say it as if there is nothing wrong with being in a room filled with people doing drugs, and/or like it is OK that the drugs are in their body even if it was acquired by passive exposure.)

If your teen does test positive for drugs and they still cling to the story that they didn't use drugs (and many of them will), then you have another option. Without arguing, simply offer to have the results confirmed at a lab using GCMS (Gas Chromatography Mass Spectrometry) technology which produces accuracy levels and results that stand up in court. To save time and unnecessary expense, you may wish to give your teen one more chance to come clean and avoid additional punishment if/when the results contradict his or her continued claims of innocence.

On a side note, a GCMS confirmation test can be a good idea if your child is on a prescription and you want to make sure they aren't abusing it. Why? Because it can tell you how much of a drug is in your teen's system, and the results are reviewed by an MRO (Medical Review Officer/Doctor). If the dosage your teen is taking is two to three times what they should be taking, then the GCMS confirmation test can reveal this. Compared to a GCMS confirmation test's ability to reveal the specific amounts of a drug in a teen's system, the home drug tests just reveal the presence or absence of a drug above a certain minimum detection threshold amount.

The minimum detection thresholds used on the best home drug test kits are set high enough that secondhand smoke and passive exposure are highly unlikely to register as positive results. It should go without saying, but I will say it anyway: If your teen tests positive on a home drug test kit, then the amount of drugs in their system isn't a good thing regardless of how the drugs got there.

What should you do if your teen refuses to take a drug test? What can you do to avoid confrontation and added stress on a relationship? The answer is an easy one. Ideally, when you first lay out the parameters of a home drug test program (rewards, consequences, options for confirmation tests, etc.), simply explain that a refusal to test will be treated as a positive result. That way, teens know in advance that there will be no debate, discussion, or unnecessary drama involved.

Stealth Options

What if you didn't set up a home drug testing program before there were any issues but you've recently noticed significant and weird changes in your teen and your gut feeling tells you it isn't typical adolescent hormones at work? What if you don't want to confront your teen and feel awkward about "calling them out" in the event that your gut feel was wrong? You've got a few options.

One option is the use of DrugWipe products. They can detect invisible drug residue on property like computer keys, televisions, and desks, etc. Results are available within minutes. Because your teen doesn't know you are investigating the presence of drug residue, concerns about adulteration or substitution are unnecessary.

Another option is the use of a private drug dog. In a conversation I had with Ray McCarty (see http://www.drugdogkc.com), he told me how many times his dog finds drugs hidden in siblings' rooms and other parts of the house besides the obvious places to look (like the user's room or automobile). And because he isn't a member of law enforcement or serving in an official capacity as such, he is not obligated to share results with anyone but the parents (or in some cases businesses) that hire him. So, results remain confidential.

If you still think there is no way your teen would ever experiment with and/or regularly use drugs, then I take no pleasure in telling you this. But if you ask parents of teens who use or used drugs, then it will be an eye-opening experience when almost all of them tell you they felt the same way before they found out the truth.

Safety by Subtraction

If you ask any police officer what percentage of crime is in some way related to drugs and/or alcohol, depending on who you talk to, expect answers from 70% to 90%. Think about it. When people are under the influence of drugs and/or alcohol, they don't think (or act) rationally and they use poor judgment. Add up the assaults, rapes, murders, domestic violence, DWI's, speeding tickets, and vandalism that happen while people are under the influence. Add up the murders and thefts associated with people buying, selling, using, or stealing to get money to buy drugs.

If your teen is able to avoid drugs, drug users, and the culture surrounding their usage, then that one move helps them bypass, sidestep, and avoid countless people and circumstances that can only bring them danger and misery. Subtract all those dangerous situations and circumstances from a lifestyle, and it becomes safer!

If you know your teens are thinking clearly (no drugs) and know who they are with and what they are really doing (both online and offline), then I'm not going to say that nothing bad can happen to them. I am saying that, along with your guidance and advice, the probability of bad things happening are about as low as you can possibly make them. And that's the whole idea.

Teens claim their parents "don't understand" or "don't know what's really going on," and in many cases they are right. Kids may not have the time and/or inclination to try and explain everything to their parents. By default, teens rely on their own judgment based on their limited life experiences.

When teens know their parents are paying attention, do understand their social circumstances, frustrations, betrayals, supporters, temptations, and have the ability to offer relevant and timely guidance, they are more likely to ask for help when they need it. They are also more likely to accept direction when they don't realize they need it.

Chapter 3:
Other People's Experience

I realize critics may claim that the idea of parents establishing rules and monitoring social media, potential drug /alcohol use, text conversations, phone conversations, where kids go, what they do, who they do it with and for how long, might seem like smothering the kids or parental overreach. I accept that criticism and it's fair.

All these tools and strategies aren't for everyone. Civilization has existed for thousands of years without the use of these tools and/or strategies. However, the risks and dangers that exist now are different from those faced by the generations that preceded us.

Please know that I have spoken with thousands of law enforcement officials, school administrators, health professionals, parents, teachers, and teens about these issues. If you want to call me closed-minded because there is nothing anyone can say to me that will make me believe that it is OK to let a seventh-grader experiment with heroin or methamphetamines, I can take it. If you want to call me a stick-in-the-mud because there is nothing anyone can say to me to make me believe that it is OK for teenagers to drive drunk, I'm not offended. And I'm not telling every parent that they need to do all of these things, all of the time, to be good parents.

I do believe that healthy relationships are facilitated by a sense of fairness. Most kids, like adults, want to be treated fairly. Kids may not like a parent's decisions, but when parents take the time to explain their rules, boundaries, and commonsense reasons for putting them in place, unnecessary conflict, mistrust, and drama can often be avoided. Parents who don't take the time to explain the "why" behind their decisions shouldn't be surprised if their teens feel they are being treated unfairly and/or become more defiant as a result.

Kids have to learn to make choices on their own. Parents can't physically be with their teens at all times as a sounding board or source of input (because of long work hours, travel, or whatever). Our goal is simply to provide parents with options, tools, and strategies that can help make their presence and influence felt in critical situations and help their children do a better job of thinking through the rewards and consequences of their choices before they make them. I choose to believe that most kids, in most circumstances, <u>will make much better choices</u> if they consider what their parents will think of their choices before they make them and ask for help if they don't know what to do.

My friend Cesar Keller, a small-business owner and parent of three kids, once told me that smart people learn from their mistakes but geniuses learn from others' mistakes. That's why we wrote this book. That's why we decided to share the following stories. That's why we hope you share these stories with others so that you and the people who matter most don't have to learn some of life's most painful lessons the hard way.

In my opinion, most parents have very little idea how much some things have changed and other things have stayed the same since they were teenagers. I say this because it has been my personal experience that they almost all say some version of the words "I had no idea" right after their teen makes a bad choice and the consequences of those choices get revealed. I see the dumbfounded and confused looks on parents' faces during speaking engagements when I clue them in to what their teens are really dealing with in school, out of school, and online.

We decided to share the following short (and true) stories to help you get a feel for what challenges you and your teens may face together or separately. In some cases, the tools and strategies mentioned earlier could have changed or prevented the outcomes. In others, maybe not. But, as you read through the stories that follow, our challenge is for you to consider all the ways the tools and strategies we've mentioned might have helped the affected families in the past and how they might help your family and others moving forward.

The challenges are real. And while some of the themes are consistent with the way teens have gotten themselves into trouble in the past (lies, substance abuse, poor choices of friends, etc.), the opportunities to get into trouble have expanded significantly because of the Internet, mobile phones, social media, and so many families with both parents working or single parents working multiple jobs to make ends meet. In any case, our goal is for you (and the other teens and parents you share these stories with) to learn from these stories rather than see them repeated.

Chapter 4:
Cyberbullying -
The Megan Meier Story

Megan Taylor Meier was born on November 6, 1992, in O'Fallon, Missouri, a suburb approximately thirty-five minutes from downtown St. Louis, Missouri. Megan weighed nine pounds, had brown curly hair, two huge dimples, and a smile that could light a room. From the moment that Megan was born, the pediatrician would show that Megan was at the top of the chart for her height and weight.

One of the first signs that Megan struggled with her self-esteem was in kindergarten. She would come home and say that the girls would tell her that her legs were too big or that she was a giant. Of course her parents would tell her to not worry about what other kids were saying because she was beautiful on the inside and outside.

In third grade, Megan was diagnosed with depression and attention-deficit hyperactivity disorder, and she began seeing a counselor and psychiatrist. Megan's fourth and fifth grade years were a little bit better, but she still struggled with friendship circles and trying to figure out how to fit in with the popular crowd.

Middle School

Megan struggled so severely with bullying in sixth and especially seventh grade that her parents decided she should switch schools for her eighth grade year. Over the summer and going into eighth grade, Megan started evolving and maturing into a beautiful young girl. She was doing really well, making new friends, joined a volleyball team, and things seemed to be going much better for her. Her parents were relieved to see Megan happy, smiling, and excited to go to school and be with her friends.

Myspace

About three weeks into her eighth grade year, Megan asked to have a Myspace account. She explained to her mom that she would be turning fourteen years old in a few months and "everyone else" already had accounts.

Megan's mom, Tina, was a protective mom. She immediately said, "Megan, no way. There are sexual predators that prey on kids." However, Megan was a very determined child and she begged for two days to have a Myspace account. Her mom, Tina, eventually broke down and told her she could have a Myspace account, but there would be rules.

Here were Tina's rules for Megan: Rule 1, only Tina had Megan's password. Rule 2, Megan's profile was to be private. Rule 3, Tina had to approve all of Megan's images and any music that she wanted to upload to her page. Rule 4, the computer was never allowed in a private space such as her room. It had to be in an open space such as the kitchen, living room, or basement. Rule 5, Tina purchased the program "Watch Right" which monitored any web pages and instant messages on the computer.

Megan wasn't thrilled with these rules. She accused her mom of acting more like the warden of a prison and complained that no other kids had parents as strict as her. Megan begrudgingly accepted the rules and started creating her Myspace account.

Because Megan was the type of girl that had struggled for so long with her self-esteem and trying to fit in with the popular crowd, her mom insisted the rules had to be in place to keep Megan from giving out too much personal information.

Approximately three weeks after Megan started her Myspace account, she received a friend request from a boy by the name of Josh Evans. Megan said, "Mom, come look at him. Can I add him, please? He's hot!" Tina asked "Do you know him?" and Megan said "No, but look at him! He's hot! Please, please, can I add him?"

Tina agreed to let her add him, but insisted that if there was anything negative or sexual in nature discussed, Megan would have to delete him immediately. Megan accepted those stipulations.

Josh's profile said he was born in Florida and recently had moved to O'Fallon. He was homeschooled. He played the guitar and drums. He was from a broken home: "When i was 7 my dad left me and my mom and my older brother and my newborn brother 3 boys God i know poor mom yeah she had such a hard time when we were younger finding work to pay for us after he left."

Megan and Josh starting talking back and forth through Myspace and AOL Instant Messenger. Josh thought Megan was cute and commented on her pictures, telling her she had beautiful eyes and a great smile. Megan thought Josh was cute and funny. As a thirteen-year-old girl, it made Megan feel great when he said nice things to her.

Tina remained vigilant and suspicious. She warned Megan to remain careful and reminded her that Josh could really be an eighty-year-old grandma or a ten-year-old kid playing a game. Megan laughed at her mom and was convinced otherwise. "Mom, I know who he is." Tina still insisted that Megan was not to give out her phone number, home address, or the school she attended.

After a span of five weeks passed, Megan and Josh were still friends. However, they didn't communicate nearly as often as they used to.

Sunday, October 15, 2006

Megan had two volleyball games that morning. Later in the afternoon, Megan asked for a ride to the store to get her birthday invitations. It was going to be her fourteenth birthday, and she was planning a huge party.

Later that evening, Megan asked if she could spend some time on Myspace while she was filling out her invitations. After being online for only a few minutes, Megan said, "Mom, come look at this." She received a message from Josh out of the blue that said, "I don't want to be friends with you anymore, you're not a nice person."

Megan was kind of confused by the message, and she didn't understand why he would send it. Megan responded and said, "Where did you get this from?" There was no response from Josh so Megan sent the message again: "Where did you get this from?" Again, there was no response from Josh. It was getting late and Megan's mom Tina told her it was time to sign off of Myspace.

Monday, October 16, 2006

Megan woke up for school and she was in a great mood. She gathered all of her birthday invitations together and out the door she went. When Tina arrived to pick Megan up from school later that day, Megan came running out of school saying, "Mom, everybody's coming to my party and it's going to be so cool."

The second Megan walked in the door at home she asked to get on Myspace to see if Josh had said anything. Tina agreed, but only for a few minutes because she had to take Megan's sister to the orthodontist.

Before Tina left, Megan got a terrible look on her face and showed her Josh's message on the computer. It said "You heard me, no one likes you. No one wants to be friends with you."

Megan was upset and asked Josh again, "Where did you get this from? I am a nice person unless somebody's mean to me first." The messages went back and forth.

Because Tina had to take Megan's sister to the orthodontist, she told Megan to sign off. Normally, Tina made sure she signed off, but because she was in a hurry, she didn't this time.

Tina called Megan two different times from the orthodontist's office. Both times, Megan was in tears because of the horrible things that were being said about her on Myspace.

Again, Tina told her to sign off. Megan didn't, and when Tina arrived home about an hour later, she was still sitting at her computer, crying.

Tina was frustrated because Megan didn't listen. Megan was hysterical.

When Tina sat down at the computer and looked at the messages going back and forth between Megan and Josh, she noticed that two other girls had joined into the conversation. The messages were humiliating, mean, and cruel. They called Megan a "fat bitch," a "whore," and plenty of other words meant to inflict pain.

Megan fought back and defended herself, but Tina tried to use this as a "teachable moment." Tina explained that a war of words never works. She pointed out how they started saying bad things about Megan and retaliation only brought Megan down to their level and escalated the situation into a huge explosion.

Tina was frustrated that Megan didn't follow her instructions, but reminded her that she was none of the things she was being called. Megan looked at her mom and said, "Who's going to believe me? It's going to everyone at my old school, everybody at my new school. Everyone is going to believe them, not me! You're supposed to be my mom, you're supposed to be on my side."

Megan immediately took off running upstairs to her room. Megan passed her dad at the top of the stairs and he asked her what was wrong, but she ran into her room. Her dad came down to the kitchen to ask Tina what was wrong with Megan and why was she so upset.

About twenty minutes later, Tina got a god-awful feeling that ran through her entire body. She stopped in mid-sentence and ran upstairs to Megan's room.

Once she opened the door, she found Megan hanging in her closet. She screamed for help and Megan's dad came running up the stairs. They worked together to get Megan down and called 911.

After what seemed like an eternity, the paramedics arrived. Even though Megan's dad and a neighbor were giving Megan CPR, it didn't seem to be working. Paramedics did get her heart started and she was able to breathe with assistance.

Megan was transported to Children's Hospital in St. Louis. However, only twenty-four hours later, on October 17, 2006, Megan Taylor Meier passed away.

Following this ordeal, Tina said, "As a parent, there is no loss like the loss of a child. It is something that absolutely transforms you the moment that your child takes their last breath. The immense amount of shock, pain, and grief take your breath away and you feel like there is no way this is happening. How did our lives change in twenty minutes? I still don't have that answer, and I don't ever think I will."

The night they left the hospital, Megan's dad went back to the house to see if Megan left a note or any other type of clue to help explain what happened and why. There was no note, but he did see on AOL Instant Messenger the last messages between Megan and Josh. Josh said, "The world would be a better place without you...have a shitty rest of your life." Megan responded by saying, "You are the kind of boy a girl would kill herself over."

Five weeks after Megan passed away and on Thanksgiving weekend, the Meiers received a call from a neighbor down the street who they didn't know very well. The neighbor asked the Meiers to attend a meeting about Megan's death. The Meiers agreed to go but were confused about what their neighbor wanted.

The meeting was at a counselor's office, and there were several people sitting in chairs in a circle. As soon as Tina Meier looked at them, she said, "So you're going to tell me that the Josh Evan's account was fake." They nodded their heads.

In fact, "Josh" was really a forty-seven-year-old woman named Lori Drew, who lived four houses down the street. Lori's thirteen-year-old daughter, Sarah, who had been friends with Megan since the fourth grade and Ashlee Grills, an eighteen-year-old family friend who worked for Lori part-time at her house, also conspired with Lori to create the Josh Evans account.

They created it because Megan and Sarah's friendship fell apart in the seventh grade. And they wanted to know if Megan was talking about Sarah behind her back now that she was in eighth grade. Their plan was to create this account, gain Megan's confidence, and see if Megan was really talking about Sarah behind her back.

Tina is confident that five weeks prior to Megan's death, the Drews had no idea that Megan was going to take her own life. They probably thought it was going to be a joke or a way to teach Megan a lesson, if in fact she was talking about Sarah behind her back.

It wasn't a joke. It was a tragedy.

Nothing could be done to bring Megan back. Knowing these three intentionally targeted Megan as a joke and there wasn't anything that the Meiers could do about it only added insult to the injuries.

The rage, anger, and sadness that the Meiers felt toward the Drews was so intense and powerful that their family members and friends encouraged the Meiers to stay away from the Drews, who only lived four houses away, for fear of revenge. They were urged to think of their younger daughter, Allison, and to use the legal system to make things right.

The Meiers contacted an attorney and the FBI. The FBI did a lengthy investigation and found that in the state of Missouri there were not any applicable laws that were broken. Lori Drew could not be charged. Missouri laws already existed related to harassment, stalking, and child endangerment, but fell short of including electronic communications in their scope. The law failed the Meiers because applicable laws weren't in place when the incidents occurred.

The Meiers had another daughter, Allison, who was ten and a half years old. Allison's life was turned upside down. Her sister was gone. And because of their grief, anger, and frustration, her parents and their relationship had changed, too.

Next, the Meiers were encouraged to get the laws changed so other parents wouldn't suffer the same fate, and they did that with the help of the media. A local journalist named Steve Poken accepted the challenge and published a story in the local paper.

The Meiers hoped the story would catch the attention of state legislators and motivate them to take the action necessary to get the laws changed. What started out as a local story quickly became international news and got the attention of the governor, who set up an Internet Task Force of which Tina Meier was asked to become a member.

Tina testified several times, and the harassment and stalking laws were amended to include electronic communications. Officially, it was Senate Bill 818, and Tina Meier was present as

Governor Matt Blunt signed it into law in August of 2008.

The Drew family has expressed no remorse for their actions and role in the events leading up to the suicide of Megan Meier. They escaped responsibility completely. Instead of focusing on things outside of her control, Tina Meier has dedicated her life to getting laws changed and making both kids and parents aware of bullying and cyberbullying so no other families suffer their fate. She created the Megan Meier Foundation (http://www.meganmeierfoundation.org) to bring awareness and the education necessary to promote positive change to children, parents, and educators about the issues surrounding bullying, cyberbullying, and suicide.

Chapter 5:
Dusting and Huffing -
The Kyle Williams Story

Jeff Williams is a police officer in a city known nationwide for its high crime rate. He works in a city with lots of gangs and drugs and at one time was ranked second in the nation in homicides per capita.

He also has a police K-9 named Thor, who was certified in drugs and general duty. Thor retired at three years old because he was shot in the line of duty and lives with Jeff. Having Thor in the house meant there was no way any members of his family or their friends could bring drugs into his house without him knowing it.

Jeff knows all about drugs. He is not naive. His wife has always asked his kids at least once a week if they've used drugs and makes them promise they won't.

As one of his favorite hobbies, Jeff likes building computers and started building a new one in February of 2005. Because he was also working on some of his older computers that were covered with dust, he made a trip to the computer store and bought a three-pack of Dust-Off.

Dust-Off is a can of compressed air made to blow dust off of a computer. A few weeks later when he went to use them, they were all empty. He talked to his kids and both of his sons said they had used them on their computers and had been messing around with them.

On February 28, he went back to the computer store. They didn't have the three-pack which he purchased before on sale so he bought a single can, jumbo size, and took it home. He set it down beside his computer.

On March 1, he left for work at 10:00 p.m. At 11:00 p.m., his wife went down and kissed his son Kyle goodnight. At 5:30 a.m. the next morning, his wife went downstairs to wake Kyle up for school before she left for work. He was sitting up in bed with his legs crossed and his head leaning over.

She called to him a few times to get up, but he didn't move. He had been known to tease her like this and pretend he fell back asleep. Even when he wasn't teasing, Kyle was never easy to wake up. So she went in and shook his arm and he fell over. He was pale white and had the straw from the Dust-Off can coming out of his mouth. He had the new can of Dust-Off in his hands. She couldn't believe it, but Kyle was dead.

Jeff is a police officer and had never heard of this. His wife is a nurse and she had never heard of this. They both found out from the coroner, after the autopsy, that it was only the propellant from the can of Dust-Off that was in Kyle's system. There were no other drugs involved, and Kyle died between midnight and 1:00 a.m.

Using Dust-Off is being done mostly by kids between the ages nine and fifteen. They even have a name for it. It's called "dusting" and it is a take-off from the Dust-Off name.

It gives people who do it a slight high for about ten seconds. It makes them dizzy. A boy who lived down the street taught Kyle how to do it about a month earlier, but Jeff and his wife never knew about it. Kyle even showed his best friend, told him it was cool and it couldn't hurt him because, after all, it was just compressed air. Fortunately, his best friend declined to participate.

Kyle was wrong. It is not just compressed air. It also contains a propellant. It's a refrigerant like what is used in your refrigerator. It is a heavy gas. It is heavier than air.

When you inhale it, it fills your lungs and keeps the good air, with oxygen, out. That's why you feel dizzy and buzzed. It decreases the oxygen to your brain and your heart.

Kyle was right. It can't hurt you. It can kill you. The horrible part about this is there is no warning. There is no level that kills you. It's not cumulative or an overdose. It can just go terribly wrong.

If you try it, it's like rolling the dice and if your number comes up you die. It's not an overdose. It's Russian roulette.

You don't die later. It's not like you don't feel good and say, "I've had too much." People usually die as they are breathing it in. You can die within two seconds of finishing "the hit." That's why the straw was still in Kyle's mouth when he died and his eyes were still open.

There is no chemical reaction or strong odor. Kyle complained a few days before he died of his tongue hurting. It probably did. The propellant causes frostbite. Jeff only wishes he had known.

Jeff and his wife have holes in their heart that can never be fixed. They say the pain of their loss is so immense they can't describe it. They can't run from their feelings of loss or hide from their grief. One of their kids won't talk about it, and the other will only sleep with Jeff and his wife.

Jeff thought his family was safe because of Thor, his knowledge of drugs, and the frequency with which he and his wife talked to his kids about drug use.

After Kyle died, another story came out about an incident at a nearby school. A probation officer went into a school building to speak with a student. While he was there, he found a student using Dust-Off in the bathroom. This student told him about another student who also had some in his locker.

This happened in a rather affluent school district. District officials told people they didn't have a drug problem there. Afterwards, rather than tell everyone about this "new" way of getting high, they tried to hide it.

Because the probation officer told the media after the news of Kyle's death, the school had no choice but to admit to it later. Jeff can only wish that he had known about it beforehand. Because if he had, it wouldn't have been in his house.

As a general rule, inhalant abuse is often more difficult to detect than other forms of substance abuse because the kids using them only need to make sure they don't get caught in the act of inhaling them. Because many popular inhalants like lighter fluid, glue, etc., are found in almost every home and are completely legal, kids often think they are harmless.

Chapter 6:
Heroin - The Sean Kilbourn and Jordan Lunsford Stories

"On Thursday, May 25, 2000, our son died...we just haven't buried him yet."

- Dave and Virgene Kilbourn

On Thursday, May 25, 2000, at the age of twenty-one, Sean Kilbourn's first shot of heroin was also his last. He took one shot of heroin and went into respiratory arrest for ten minutes.

At 8:43 a.m. Eastern Time on that day, Sean's parents received a phone call from a Brownsburg, Indiana, policeman who told them their son Sean was found clinically dead at a friend's apartment. He had been rushed to the emergency room in a neighboring town and was in critical condition on life support. "Was it an accident?" they asked. There was a pause and then came an unbelievable answer, "No, it was a heroin overdose."

Then they got hit with all the questions:

"Did Sean have a history of drug use?" No!

"Were they aware of any drug use?" No!

"Were there any unusual changes in his behavior?" No!

"Was there anyone in the family with a history of drug or alcohol abuse?" No!

"Were there any suicide attempts?" No!

"What was he doing in Indiana?" He was visiting friends.

"Did any of his friends do drugs?" Not that they were aware of.

When Virgene visited with the doctor, she was told in a very solemn voice, "You need to get here right away." Virgene explained that she was living in Michigan and waiting for her husband to get home before they could leave and make the four-hour trip.

Before she left, she had to ask, "Are you sure this is Sean?"

The doctor informed her that it was. She couldn't believe it. Why would he try heroin? It was so out of character for him. He had always been a bright, gifted student who excelled in all subjects. He was industrious and worked hard at his job.

When they reached the hospital, they hurried to the ICU and tried to prepare themselves. A nurse greeted them, showed them to the room, and explained what they were going to see.

Sean was on life support. A machine was breathing for him. There were many tubes and an IV. The doctors suspected brain damage had already occurred.

When they got their first look, they saw their son in a coma with his eyes closed and face swollen. The breathing apparatus was taped to his head and mouth. His heart monitor was registering 180 beats per minute. When the normal rate for most healthy children his age is usually in the seventies. There was also some damage to his heart muscle from the aggressive CPR.

He was found clinically dead with no heartbeat or blood pressure according to his doctor. Upon further examination for marks, the only injection point they discovered was between the big toe and the next toe.

The next day they found out the results of the electroencephalogram (the test that shows brain activity). The prognosis was grim. Only his most basic life instincts existed.

A few more days passed by with no progress. Sean needed a tracheotomy and a feeding tube to survive.

After a few weeks, he was still in a coma and they were told that they needed to find a long-term-care nursing facility because Sean could not remain in the hospital indefinitely. So, in August of 2000, Sean was moved to a nursing home. He was by far (at least several decades) the youngest resident. His parents, Dave and Virgene, were heartbroken.

Many years have passed since Sean's overdose, and he remains trapped in a persistent, vegetative state.

Although he looks normal, despite the wheelchair, he has yet to speak. He just smiles, makes noises, and laughs occasionally. He has endured numerous infections and has been hospitalized over thirty times. At one point he had lost forty pounds.

Out of the blue several years ago, he started having seizures. Sometimes he would have them several times a day.

When Sean had his thirtieth birthday, Dave and Virgene couldn't help but to reflect on all their family had been through. This needless tragedy didn't just happen to Sean and affect his life forever; it changed theirs, too.

Little did Dave and Virgene know that from that day forward, they would be spending a large portion of each day (six to seven hours) with Sean at a nursing home. They want Sean to feel their presence and know somehow that they are there for him, after the incident, just like they were there for him before. Instead of leaving him in a nursing home, forgetting about him, and moving on with their lives, they continue to stay attached, because he is their son and they love him.

The Jordan Lunsford story has a different ending. Jordan was always a little rough around the edges. Growing up, he was smaller than his peers, and wore braces and glasses, too. Because he stood up for himself, he got in lots of fights when people tried picking on him or making fun of him.

What people didn't know was that he also suffered from mental illness. He was, in fact, bipolar.

After initially being misdiagnosed with attention deficit hyperactivity disorder, the doctors recognized the mistake and put him on a treatment plan that seemed to be working. For a while things were starting to look up.

Because Jordan's parents had been addicts for a good portion of their lives, when it came to drugs, they were cautious. They would check on Jordan concerning this periodically, and occasionally found slight traces of marijuana. When that occurred, they addressed it immediately.

Sadly, two weeks after he turned seventeen years old, his pregnant mother found a note in his place. It read that Jordan had left home. He did not wish to live by their rules. He did not want to be held accountable by his family. He reminded them that legally nothing could be done about his decision, and that he believed it was best for him.

Shortly after leaving home, Jordan quit school. He moved to Texas to live with his biological father who had not been a part of his life at all since he was two years old. While away from home, he began using more drugs.

Thankfully, he did return from Texas. When he came back, he made the effort to better communicate with his mother. He would even stay over some nights.

In support of his efforts to change, his parents tried to help him get into an alternative school. While filling out his paperwork, Jordan experienced extreme frustration. His stepfather corrected his attitude and pointed out that if he couldn't handle paperwork, how could he handle being back in school? Jordan was only home for about two weeks before he walked right back out the door.

After he left, Jordan and his mother spoke every night. After some time had passed, Jordan's mother got him to agree to come home once again. He told her she could pick him up the next evening at five o'clock. When she went to pick him up at their meeting place, Jordan was not there. She called the house where he had been staying, and they said he had left and not been seen since.

Her husband was with their four-year-old picking up steak to cook for dinner. She called him and sadly said, "I guess Jordan isn't coming." His immediate reply was, "What are you talking about? I just saw him." Jordan had been at the store, and he personally informed his father that he would indeed be coming to dinner. Jordan hugged his sibling and left.

At dinner time, they made his plate and waited, and waited, and waited. Finally, his mother fell asleep. It turned out that Jordan called her a little past midnight after she had fallen asleep and left a typical message.

A few hours later, her phone started ringing like crazy. She was told there was an emergency and that she needed to get to the hospital. No one would tell her why on the other end.

Jordan overdosed on heroin. The people he was with drove him to St. Louis (which was a considerable distance) once they recognized something was wrong. They made the long trip to St. Louis rather than call 911 because they didn't want to get in trouble with the law.

By the time the hospital took him in, it took forty minutes to get his heart working again. Jordan went on life support, and was pronounced brain-dead the very next day.

His parents made the grueling decision to donate Jordan's organs, and Jordan saved many lives that day. But he lost his own. His mother walked into the waiting room and had to tell the rest of his family that Jordan was gone. The hospital staff allowed her to stay with him. When they were ready to transfer him for the organ donations, she helped them wrap him up to keep him warm from the cold outside. Once he was inside the ambulance, she let him go.

That was the last time his mother got to feel his skin warm with life.

Jordan's mother started a foundation in his honor. She called it Jordan's Place. It is a sanctuary for teens dealing with issues like drug abuse to come and talk to someone about it and receive the help they need. The location of their building is one block away from where Jordan overdosed.

In this area, there have been many deaths since Jordan's. Every time his mother hears about one, it feels like the day he died all over again. She had no idea heroin was such a problem. She says that she will never be okay again, and there is no getting used to not seeing your children. She wants people to know that it was only one line of heroin that ended her son's life. Just one. That's all it takes. Sometimes, a "onetime thing" is also the last thing one ever does.

Jordan's mother wishes she would have known they had a problem in the first place. No one in their town ever talked about what was happening with their teens and drugs. No one ever mentioned that there was an ongoing battle with drugs in their neighborhood.

If you want to learn more about Jordan's Place, visit www.jordansplace-mo.org.

Chapter 7:
Date Rape, Sexting, Underage Drinking, Bullying, and Suicide - The Rehtaeh Parsons Story

Rehtaeh's life was forever changed one dreaded night in November of 2011. Like many teenagers, Rehtaeh joined a girlfriend for a weekend sleepover. Her friend suggested they visit two teenage boys that lived close by and went to their school. So they walked over and hung out with them until two other boys arrived—with vodka.

They all passed the bottle around and everyone drank their fair share, including Rehtaeh. Like many other kids at age fifteen, she wasn't experienced with the effects or power of alcohol. She drank too much, became disoriented, and described the night afterwards as a blur.

That night she was raped by four boys. To make matters worse, one of the boys took a photo of her being raped and distributed the photo to other kids at school and members of her community.

What did the photo show? It showed her with her head hanging out a window, vomiting, while one of the four boys, naked from the waist down, was pressed into her from behind. In the photo, the boy raping her posed and gave a thumbs-up.

The photo quickly went viral, and as a victim of rape, she was shunned by almost everyone she knew. She was harassed and bullied on Facebook and via text messages. The harassment became so bad that she moved away and tried to get a fresh start in a new community.

As a result, she struggled emotionally with depression and anger. She had thoughts of suicide and was placed in the local hospital in an attempt to get help. She stayed in the hospital for six weeks.

When she eventually moved back to her community, all was not forgotten. Her victimization continued long after the initial rape.

In August of 2012, approximately nine months after the night she was raped, local police concluded their investigation and explained to Rehtaeh and her parents that there was a lack of evidence and that they would not be pressing charges against any of the four boys.

During the initial investigation, none of the four boys were interviewed. Their cell phones were not seized for evidence. Her parents were told that the photo being distributed of their daughter being raped was a "community matter."

Rehtaeh continued to receive harassment and cyberbullying. She turned to drugs and self-harm as a way to cope.

She had no interest in school and couldn't bring herself to attend regularly. Counseling didn't work either. She felt despair and hopelessness. The pain of the rape and her disappointment in others she thought she could count on were simply too much. She took her own life in April of 2013. She died at the age of seventeen with her loved ones by her side.

For additional information on Rehtaeh and her story, see the Rehtaeh Parsons Society at http://rehtaehparsons.ca.

Chapter 8:
Texting and Driving - The Alex Brown Story

On November 10, 2009, Johnny Mac and Jeanne Brown lost their eldest daughter, Alex, who was seventeen and a senior at Seagraves High School in Texas. Alex died one tragic morning on her way to school because she was texting, driving, and not wearing her seatbelt. The accident happened when she veered off the road, rolled her truck, and was thrown from her vehicle.

The event came as a surprise to the Browns, who had just had a conversation with their daughter a week prior to the accident about the dangers of texting while driving. They explained to her that "it takes six seconds to read, analyze, and respond to a text. At 70 mph, that's like driving a football field and a half."

"Even after I buried my seventeen-year-old daughter, I found myself driving with (this Blackberry) in my ear," Johnny Mac Brown said. Johnny Mac described his cellphone as a "Crackberry" and said he was just as addicted to it as a drug addict is to drugs. Since then he has been on a campaign to encourage others to stop using their cellphones when driving, too.

When Jeanne Brown gets the opportunity to speak with young drivers about texting, driving, and the possibilities of death, she lets them know that in addition to losing their daughter, they racked up over $150,000 in medical bills after Alex's death. To drive the point home even further, she asks students and young drivers to tell their parents what type of funeral they want, what they want to be buried in, and what they want on their headstones.

Is talking to your kids enough? The Browns would probably argue otherwise. If your teen pushes limits and doesn't think bad things can happen to them, what other things can you do to inspect the responsible and lifesaving behavior you expect? Are dash cams and periodic spot checks necessary to ensure compliance with your "no texting and driving" rules? Is it necessary to spot-check your teen's text messages, Facebook entries, tweets, and Instagram posts, etc., during times when you knew they were driving?

Chapter 9:
Sexting and Bullying -
The Amanda Todd Story

Amanda Michelle Todd killed herself at the age of fifteen at her home in <u>Port Coquitlam</u>, British Columbia, Canada. She was a sophomore at CABE Secondary in Coquitlam, which was a school that catered to students who experienced social and behavioral issues in previous educational settings.

The beginning of her end started three years earlier when she was only in seventh grade. She had recently moved in with her father and used video chat rooms to meet new people over the Internet. After receiving numerous compliments on her looks, a stranger, after a year of trying, finally convinced her to bare her breasts on her computer's webcam.

The stranger then blackmailed Amanda with threats of making her topless photo available to her friends unless she gave him a "show." He said he knew her "address, school, friends, and family names."

At 4:00 a.m., during Christmas break, Amanda got a knock on the door. It was the police. They informed her that her photo had been sent "everywhere" and was circulating on the Internet.

The cyberbullying and sexual exploitation caused anxiety, depression, and panic disorders so severe that her family moved and she began using drugs and alcohol.

A year later, the stranger reappeared. He created a profile on Facebook using her topless photograph as the profile image. Then he devised a way to begin contacting her new classmates at her new school so they all saw it, too.

The stranger would go online and find kids who went to her new school. He would reach out to them and tell him he was going to be a new student the following week and that he looked forward to making new friends. He then asked them if they would accept his friend's request on Facebook.

After the stranger gathered enough names, he would send Amanda's video and pictures to her new school. Again, she lost her friends and respect. She sat at lunch, alone. Teasing followed and Amanda changed schools once again.

She knew she could never get that picture back. She also knew what that meant.

Soon "an old guy friend" contacted her, led her on, and made her believe he liked her. He invited Amanda to his house and they had sex while his girlfriend was on vacation. His girlfriend found out upon her return. Her "old guy friend" along with his girlfriend and about fifteen of her friends confronted Amanda at school. The girlfriend and two other girls said, "Look around. Nobody likes you," in front of her new school with fifty people watching.

Next a guy in the crowd yelled, "Punch her already." So the girlfriend pushed her to the ground and let the punches fly while the group of bystanders filmed it, and harassed and taunted Amanda even further.

The girlfriend and her group of friends left Amanda lying injured in the ditch. That ditch is exactly where Amanda's father found her.

Following the attack, Amanda attempted to commit suicide by drinking bleach. She was taken to the hospital. Her stomach was pumped and she survived.

When Amanda got home, she returned to discover abusive and hateful messages about her failed suicide attempt posted on Facebook.

"Did you wash the mud out of your hair?"

"She deserved it."

"I hope she's dead."

Six months after the incident, people were still posting pictures of Clorox, bleach, and ditches.

"I hope she uses a different bleach next time."

"I hope she dies this time and isn't so stupid."

"I hope she sees this and kills herself."

By March of 2012, she felt she was unable to escape her past. Her anxiety was so bad she wouldn't go outside or leave her house.

Amanda's mental state got worse and her self-esteem kept plummeting. Before long she began self-mutilation (cutting).

She was prescribed antidepressants and received counseling, but nothing seemed to provide significant relief. After an overdose of her prescription medicine, she was hospitalized for two days and things went from bad to worse upon her return.

Her grades suffered. The kids started calling her "psycho" and teasing her for spending so much time in what they referred to as a "crazy hospital."

Prior to Amanda's suicide on October 10, 2012, she was a sophomore in high school and posted a video on YouTube in which she used a series of flash cards to tell her story. It went viral (over seventeen million views) after her death and generated media attention on an international scale.

As a result of her death, a national discussion on the criminalization of cyberbullying took place in Canada. Government officials took action to propose funding and support for anti-bullying organizations. Amanda's mother, Carol, established the Amanda Todd Trust (http://www.amandatoddlegacy.org) as a way of receiving donations to support anti-bullying awareness education as well.

Chapter 10:
Drinking and Driving -
The Michael Glynn Story

Michael Glynn was a typical high school senior. Because he didn't like being cooped up in a classroom all day, he wasn't a big fan of school, even though he had his favorite classes and teachers.

His preference was being outside. He loved hunting, fishing, riding, rodeo riding, and even working, as long as he was outside.

He went to school every day, and sat in those classrooms, because he knew it would get him to the point in his life where he could make his own choices. He looked forward to continuing his education the following year at Chadron State in Nebraska and studying things he was actually interested in learning more about.

He wanted to be on their rodeo team, and he was going to study range management. After college, he wanted to return home and work with his dad on his family's ranch. Those were his future plans, and his parents were thrilled for him.

Michael graduated from White River High School on Sunday, May 14, 2006. That was probably the most important day of his life. Understand that May is a busy month on a ranch, and there are really no "days off." His family was planning on moving their cattle to a different pasture the morning after graduation to get ready for branding calves later in the week.

Sunday night, after they celebrated Michael's graduation with their extended and immediate family, Michael was getting ready to leave and continue celebrating with his buddies. Knowing he would be expected to help move the cattle, he asked his dad what time they were going to start and when he should be home that night. He also added, "You know, we are going to have alcohol at the party."

His parents knew the kids would be drinking that night, and they knew Michael had done so before. Normally, when they found out he had been drinking, they would punish him by grounding him, taking his car away from him, giving him extra chores, or whatever they could do to deter his underage drinking.

But that night, after reaching such an important milestone in his life, they didn't tell him to not drink. They knew he would anyway, so they told him what they thought at the time was the best and safest alternative.

Michael's father said, "Michael, we know you guys are all going to be drinking tonight, and we just want you to be safe. So let's forget about moving cows tomorrow morning; we'll do it in the afternoon or the next day. We just don't want you to drive home tonight. Stay at the party, or stay at your friend's house or in town. Just don't be driving."

Michael was shocked to hear those words escape his dad's mouth. It was something he never heard before and never expected to hear. He was pretty excited. He had just been given permission to go out and celebrate and drink, as long as he didn't drive. He promised he would stay at his friend's house all night.

As he walked down the driveway to his car, he looked back at his parents, waved, and said, "Okay, see you tomorrow afternoon." Those were the last words they ever heard Michael say.

Early the next morning, as his brother and mother were headed to town for school and work, the sheriff pulled up to their house. He told them Michael had been in an accident, and that they needed to get to the hospital quickly.

The hospital was in a town about sixty miles away. As they journeyed, Michael's mother formed a hatred for her son's friends. She didn't know which one it was, but she just knew it was one of them that had been driving and wrecked and hurt Michael. She knew that because they had told Michael not to drive and he had promised he wouldn't.

When they were about eight miles from White River, they saw his car in the ditch. It was terrible. It was at that moment that his mother knew Michael had attempted to drive home.

The thought kept going through her mind: "Why?" She longed to know once they knew Michael was all right. She never did get her answers from her son.

Whether he fell asleep or passed out was never determined. But they do know that his blood alcohol level was 0.16, which is twice the legal limit for an adult over the age of twenty-one.

He had been driving home alone at about six o'clock that morning. The car drifted into the ditch, where it hit an approach at a speed estimated around eighty mph. The car became airborne, and when it landed, it rolled several times. Michael was not wearing a seatbelt and was thrown from the car.

When they reached the hospital, they saw Michael lying on a table. He looked like he was asleep. He had a few grass stains on his blue jeans, but other than that he seemed to be in fair condition. The doctors gave them the good news that he had no broken bones and no significant cuts or lacerations. They thought that was a miracle!

There were concerns related to internal bleeding, so they wanted him flown to Sioux Falls for further treatment immediately. Michael's father flew with him in the air ambulance, and Matt, his brother, and his mother made the five-hour drive to Sioux Falls.

When they arrived in Sioux Falls later that day, Michael was still in a coma and the doctors had been running tests nonstop.

The next day, the doctor told the family that there had actually been no significant damage to his organs, but that he had experienced severe brain damage. In the next ten seconds, his mother's mind raced. "Wow," she thought. "He might not be able to start college this fall. He might not even be able to rodeo this summer. He might have to relearn how to walk and talk. We'll probably have to get a wheelchair ramp built going into the house."

Then the doctor said the words that forever burned into her mind: "And that's the injury that is going to take his life." For a split second, she thought, "Okay. Many, many years from now it can take his life." But then the doctor said, "It may happen today, or tomorrow, or next week. We're not sure, but it will be soon."

The doctors and nurses told them that shortly before he would die, his brain would hemorrhage. They told them what some of those signs would be, mostly by explaining what the monitors he was hooked up to would be showing. They said when what they explained happened, he would be very near to his death.

The next morning they noticed that Michael's eyes were about halfway opened. They were so excited! But he wasn't blinking. The nurses said that he had lost his ability to keep his eyes closed. His brain was literally shutting down.

Later that same morning, with a room full of Michael's friends with him, one of his legs jerked slightly when a nurse was doing one of the tests. Again, their excitement grew. They just knew that was the miracle they had been praying for. Michael was going to come around.

Roger and Joyce, Michael's parents, sat there quietly. His mother commented to the nurse, "That wasn't a good sign, was it?" The nurse replied, "No." It was actually a sign that his brain was beginning to hemorrhage. His dad and mom sat there with him alone, for a few more hours, until the monitors showed them the dreaded numbers. The doctors performed their final tests, ending with the declaration that Michael had died.

Michael's parents told Michael when he was sober not to drive and he readily agreed. However, alcohol can make people feel relaxed and invincible. People do things they would have never done while sober (like pick fights with a friend, stumble around, etc.). It impairs judgment.

Alcohol told Michael, "You're fine. You've driven that road home hundreds of times. You know it like the back of your hand. You're tough. You'll be fine." Well, the alcohol lied. And Michael died.

Michael spent thirteen years going to school, sitting in a classroom each day, because he had no choice; because he knew that it would lead to the time in his life when he could choose what he wanted to do, what he wanted to study, what he wanted to be, and what he wanted to do with his life. And as soon as he got to that point it was all for nothing, because he made the choice to drink and drive that night.

In Michael's case, he doesn't have to live with the consequences of his choice to drink and drive that night. But his friends and family do. And they have to live every day knowing that they condoned his drinking that night and played a role in his death, too.

Michael's mother wishes she would have been more knowledgeable about the true danger and effects of alcohol. She and her husband had always thought, in the back of their mind, that drinking was a rite of passage for kids. Michael would grow out of it. They were the type to think that bad things only happened to the kids who drank and lived far away — that it wouldn't happen to them.

Chapter 11:
Synthetic Drugs and High-Speed Driving - The Max Dobner Story

Max Dobner drove his car into a house in Batavia, Illinois, and died. Reports after the incident indicated he was driving on streets in residential areas at speeds between 80-100 mph before he crashed and his life ended.

Max called his older brother thirty minutes before his accident to report that he had "smoked that legal stuff," meaning synthetic marijuana. He said his heart was really pounding and he was "freaking out." His brother told him to lie down and he would be okay. Unfortunately, his brother had no idea what kind of hallucinations and paranoid delusions Max was experiencing.

Shortly after the incident, Max's mother, Karen, got the phone call explaining what had happened. She said, "I knew that something had happened when the officer told me that Max had run out of the house and left all the doors open and let the animals out. Max had always been so responsible and conscientious. He would have never left the house open like that."

It turns out that before this incident, Max told one of his friends that because marijuana was illegal and this wasn't, it had to be safer. He was wrong.

Karen Dobner has since made it her business to learn everything she possibly could about synthetic cannabinoids used to make synthetic marijuana or "poison sprayed on leaves," as she calls it. What she found out is that synthetic marijuana causes seizures, hallucinations, vomiting, paranoid delusions, anxiety and panic attacks, organ failure (usually kidneys), rapid heart rate, body temperature fluctuations, temporary inability to feel pain, depression, psychosis, exaggerated thoughts of suicide and homicide, feelings of impending doom, heart attacks, and death.

Within a week of Max's death, she decided to start a foundation in Max's honor (http://www.2themax.org) to advocate for education and legislation in her crusade against the use of synthetic marijuana. She has remained vigilant helping victims, educating others, and advocating for effective legislation in an attempt to minimize unnecessary incidents in the future.

Because of her work and that of Illinois Attorney General Lisa Madigan, law enforcement agents, and Illinois legislators, it's not as easy to find the synthetic drugs in stores next to the bubble gum and candy bars as it used to be in Illinois.

Chapter 12:
Mixing Prescription Drugs, Alcohol, and Peer Pressure - The Dustin Babcock Story

Dustin Babcock is dead. The eighteen-year-old's heart stopped after a late night of partying with prescription drugs and alcohol. Here's how the cause of death was listed in his autopsy report: "Toxic effects of Tramadol," a drug prescribed for pain. "Manner of death: accidental."

No one believes Dustin wanted to die. Days before his death he had written letters to family and friends admitting and regretting the many poor choices he had made. He wrote that he had rededicated his life to God.

The small, tow-headed boy was in the fourth grade when he came to live with his grandparents Nedra and Terry Babcock. The Babcocks said Dustin was playful and often joked around. He wanted to please people but also would stand up for himself when challenged.

He had a head for math and science and began taking calculus at Evangelistic Temple School when in middle school. The Babcocks loved Dustin in the best way they knew and even adopted him legally as their own. They always felt he was looking for a love he could never find, in spite of their best efforts to express it.

In the ninth grade, Dustin got in with a trouble-making crowd, a circle of kids who used drugs and drank. Dustin followed their lead. He smoked marijuana, missed curfew, skipped school, and eventually got arrested for more-serious crimes.

The Babcocks grounded Dustin. They took away his privileges and sought family counseling along with him.

For short periods of time, Dustin's choices and behaviors would improve, but then the allure of the wrong crowd appealed to him too much, so it didn't take long before he found himself reliving the same destructive lifestyle that had gotten him into trouble before.

The Babcocks were at a loss when it came to ideas of what they could do about it because, up to this point, nothing they tried worked.

Before sunrise, on a warm day in May of 2003, the Babcocks felt they had no other choice but to wake up their fifteen-year-old, have him handcuffed - for his safety and theirs - and taken to the Agape Boarding School in Stockton, Missouri, four and a half hours away.

They expected a fight and they got it. Dustin kicked, screamed, and cried. "He had left us no alternative. His life was in a downward spiral," said Terry.

Reports indicated that it only took a few weeks for his attitude to change. He came home a year later and even spoke of his reformation at church.

Shortly after Dustin's return, Nedra threw him a birthday party at Fajita Rita's, where she remembers looking at Dustin, a short, blue-eyed teenager with spiked hair, and thinking the worst was over. "It was so fun," she said. "We were convinced (he was cleaned up) or else we wouldn't have brought him home. But it's tough out there."

Dustin returned to his defiant ways about a year later. In May of 2005, he was arrested on drug-related charges. He had gotten into far greater trouble than the Babcocks could ever had suspected.

Dustin was arrested again September 24, 2005, for possession of marijuana and methamphetamine with the intent to distribute. He also acquired a record for burglary and larceny.

This time the Babcocks didn't bail Dustin out until a week after his arrest. During that week in jail, Dustin wrote down his thoughts in letters he wrote to his family.

He had intentions: "I plan to pick a new set of friends because the ones I have aren't helping me achieve my goals in life."

He had hopes: To be a dentist and "live a good life, away from drugs and sin."

He had regrets: "Mom (Nedra), I love you so dearly and am so sorry for the hurt I've caused....You are the sunshine in my life."

Terry bailed Dustin out of jail on September 30, and later that evening Dustin went to the fair with his girlfriend. His curfew was 11:00 p.m., but Dustin didn't make it home, ever.

The following evening, a policeman had come to the Babcock's door. He explained that Dustin was found in a nonresponsive state by a female friend at her house between noon and 1:00 p.m. that day, and he died shortly after arriving at the hospital, according to the autopsy report. Dustin had a large amount of Tramadol and mixed it with alcohol. The combination was lethal.

Chapter 13:
The Choking Game, Fainting, and Knockout - The Josh Jarman and Erik Robinson Stories

Neecy Jarman came home from work one day to find her son had died at the age of thirteen. Of course, some people suspected suicide because he was found with a cord wrapped around his neck.

When Neecy began connecting the dots, she knew better. A kid planning on committing suicide doesn't usually fold clothes to earn an extra $20 in spending money so he can hang out with his friends the next day. A kid planning on committing suicide doesn't put away leftover ribs so he can have them for lunch the next day. He was found seated on the floor, and he had plenty of room to move around. If he was really trying to commit suicide, the evidence just didn't back that up.

If not suicide, what did happen? After the fact, Neecy did some digging on Facebook and discovered that he was talking about and involved in playing a game he called "knockout" which is a variation of the choking game that usually is played in groups. She talked to some of his friends and learned that Josh learned how to play by himself. His cause of death was no longer a mystery.

The goal of the "game" is to cut off the supply of oxygen to the brain and experience a fainting and euphoric state as a result. Sometimes it involves placing things like a belt, cord, arms, or hands around an individual's neck so there is compression on the carotid artery. Other variations involve forced overbreathing and hyperventilation followed by holding his or her breath and being bear-hugged around the chest, which causes a feeling of euphoria then dizziness.

Neecy had never heard of this game before the passing of her son. But she found out later that her experience was not unique and that other parents had similar experiences as a result of their kids "playing" this "game." There is even a choking game awareness ribbon and choking game awareness day, which unites parents who have already suffered and warns parents who otherwise might not be aware of the dangers.

Kids think it's a game. Parents who don't know any better think it's a game, too. Unfortunately, it often ends in broken bones, brain damage, and sometimes, as in the case of Josh Jarman, death.

Judy Rogg, executive director and founder of Erik's Cause (http://www.erikscause.org), lost her twelve-year-old son, Erik Robinson, to the choking game in April of 2010. Judy founded a nonprofit organization, recruited subject experts, and developed a non-graphic, skills-based curriculum to educate other parents, schools, and communities about the hazards of the choking game and to prevent others from experiencing her personal tragedy.

Pass-out activities (most commonly known as the choking game) are generations old and know no boundaries. They injure and kill children of all races, religions, and socioeconomic groups children both considered "at risk" and also the antithesis of "at risk." Little has been publicized about it, and when incidents are reported, officials are quick to dismiss it because of poor statistics. But statistics do not tell the story as there are no injury or death codes to accurately gather this data.

With the rise of YouTube and easy access to information about these games on the Internet, local children can learn about this from kids half the world away, thinking it is harmless fun. They have no idea of the dangers.

Erik's Cause was founded to stop preventable injuries and deaths from these activities through skills-based education. The main goal was to help kids and parents understand potential dangers without arousing curiosity. Secondary goals included providing ways to help kids say "no" to peer pressure and other risky behaviors.

Their mission is to bring awareness of the deadly choking game into the national spotlight so parents and children understand its true dangers and lives can be saved. They believe education is the most effective way to combat its rampant popularity.

Their program is twofold: (1) It engages students in an interactive dialogue about basic brain science and what happens in the brain when its function is interrupted by these "games" using straightforward, honest facts, and (2) it builds skills to say "no" to peer pressure, which is particularly difficult during the teen years when everyone wants to fit in with their peers.

Chapter 14:
Conclusion -
Ready for the Real World

While some critics condemn some of the tools and strategies discussed in this book as being overprotective, unnecessary, and complicit in leaving kids grossly unprepared for adulthood and their own decision making in the real world, we would argue the opposite. Here's why:

If kids undergo home drug testing in order to continue receiving their privileges at home, how is that different from an adult in the real world undergoing drug testing at work in order to continue receiving the privileges of employment? If a teen has his or her text communications and/or computer activity monitored at home, how is that any different from working at a company that monitors computer usage and phone conversations "for training purposes" at work? If a teen is given driving rules and they are monitored by GPS, how is that different from an adult who drives a company vehicle on delivery routes (like a UPS driver) that is monitored by GPS so as to deter unnecessary breaks, detours, or unsafe driving?

Like parents, businesses recognize that there is plenty of room for people to use their own discretion, make their own choices, and learn from them. Like parents, successful businesses also realize there are certain activities and behaviors that are simply too risky to allow. And they have implemented tools, technologies, and rules to mitigate those risks.

Successful businesses fall in love with their bottom line and protect it as best they can. Parents love their children and are learning and exploring new ways to protect them as best they can. We wrote this book and shared these ideas because we don't believe businesses care more about their bottom line than parents do about their kids.

Our goal was never to tell you how to parent. It was to give you a smorgasbord of ideas, strategies, tips, and tools that have helped other parents solve some of their biggest potential challenges before they occurred. It was to inspire you to remain alert to dangers facing your teens on any given day regardless of how much you've "talked to your teens" about them. It was to inspire you to gather the information you need to make better decisions faster and take appropriate action where necessary. We wish you and your family the best!

Bonus Section:
The Next Step -
A Community Solution

Maybe you and your teens have got it all together. Maybe your kids really don't engage in any risky teen behaviors. Maybe they always tell the truth and don't go anywhere or do anything they aren't supposed to without you knowing about it. Maybe they know all the do's and don'ts related to online safety and never view or type anything they might regret later.

Unfortunately, they go to school with and interact with other kids who don't have it together and don't make good choices. They go to school with lots of kids who make bad choices often. Some of the bad choices (especially made under the influence of drugs and/or alcohol) can affect your kids, too. What, if anything, can you and/or other parents and community leaders do to make a community better and safer regardless of funding or the availability of people in positions of public service?

I'm going to attempt to provide your community with a simple solution to a complex problem. In doing so, I'd like to share a story made famous in a book called Awaken the Giant Within, by Tony Robbins, many years ago. I think this book really illuminates a common-sense approach to making communities stronger and safer.

In his book, Robbins told the story of a man who was standing on the shores of a river. As the man looked out across the water, he saw someone struggling to swim and screaming for help. He dove in, made a daring rescue, and pulled the drowning victim to safety. He lay on the beach, exhausted, only to look up and see two more people hollering for help. He dove in, pulled both to safety, and was completely exhausted. All of his energy was spent. The second he looked up, he saw four more people coming down the stream screaming for help.

The moral of the story is that if he had just taken the time to walk a short distance upriver, he would have discovered the one person throwing all these people in the river in the first place and saved all his time, energy, and resources addressing a single cause upriver instead of the many effects downriver.

What single cause creates a ton of problems downriver for school leaders, politicians, law enforcement, parents, and teens? Drugs. Want some ideas on how to solve those problems before they occur? Here you go!

The Model of 911 Emergency Services

Not long ago, some people got together with a common goal and a simple idea to execute it. They wanted everyone to know what to do in case of an emergency. If someone fell down on the ground right now in front of you and stopped breathing, chances are you would know what to do, your kids would know what to do, and so would your neighbors. Call 911, right?

We all know that. We also know that there are systems set up behind the scenes that will get help to arrive as soon as possible. But you don't have to worry about that. All you have to do is remember to call 911.

It's simple. It works.

Well, what if there was an idea that was almost as simple as dialing 911 in an emergency that every community could execute right now, with the back-end support and funding already in place that could help get drugs out of our homes, schools, and communities and keep them out?

What if instead of making a phone call, parents could just visit a website, like your town's website, your police department's website, or your school district's website, to be more specific, and just click on a link instead?

Well that's exactly what I'm going to share with you. Over the years, I've spoken to thousands of parents, teens, law enforcement officials, school board members, superintendents, principals, politicians, prosecuting attorneys, coalition leaders, and even a few former drug dealers.

With the exception of the drug dealers, they all shared a common goal: to keep the kids in their families and communities from using illegal

94

drugs. In varying capacities, they all work to achieve those goals.

Community leaders all have different reasons for wanting to keep kids from using drugs. The police know what percentage of crimes are related to substance abuse in one way or another (theft, assaults, murders, etc.), and it's a high number. Schools know that safety, test scores, attendance, and dropout rates are related to substance abuse. Politicians know that their reelection can be affected by community problems related to drugs and substance abuse. Parents know that their kids' lives, their lives, and their property values are affected by substance abuse issues.

You know what else they all share in common? It's a lack of time. They're all busy, and every time someone says to them that they just need a minute of your time or need to run something quick by them, they all know better. It's not going to take a minute or be something quick. It's going to take a bunch of time.

That's a big part of why I'm convinced many drug prevention efforts in the past have fallen short of objectives. Because until now, most of the common prevention strategies and ideas weren't designed to work in stride with these busy people, as part of what they were already doing, without creating more work or placing additional demands on their time.

But what if there was a way to solve these community problems related to drugs without interfering with the busy lives of the local leaders? Or better yet, what if there was a way to make things easier and create less work and fewer hassles? There is and I'll explain it.

Here's the thing: If you talk to these people, they all have different ideas about how to solve the problems or at least make them smaller. And I do think that the individual efforts of these people do make a difference. However, I also believe that most of them, if they're honest, will tell you that even if they are doing all they can with what they have, they still know it isn't enough.

Who's right? Do the police need to make more arrests? Do the prosecutors need to even get tougher sentences? Do the schools and community coalitions need to do a better job educating students on the dangers of drugs and substance abuse? Do we need more treatment centers? Do parents need to pay closer attention to their children and communicate their drug-free expectations?

They're all right. We do need more of all those things, but if you look at things from the perspective of the leaders in these positions, there are some legitimate reasons why they can't and don't happen.

They don't always have the time, money, or political support they need. Maybe they can't risk losing their jobs or in some cases their lives. Without knowing the details of their lives, I can't blame them or judge them.

What I'd rather do is help. Suppose you're a concerned citizen and you demand that the police arrest all the drug dealers in your community, and they do. Then you demand that the prosecutors prosecute them all to the fullest extent of the law. Then what? One of two things happens.

The small-time amateur criminal goes away to state prison and gets out as a big-time professional criminal and then returns to your community a bigger threat than he or she was before they got arrested in the first place. Or the prisons get filled up and the judges have no choice but to offer probation and all you've done is wasted the time of the law enforcement officials and prosecutors because the drug dealer is back in your community in no time.

I have developed great relationships with volunteer and professionally trained community coalition leaders who give everything of themselves to support the drug-free efforts of their communities. They are friends of mine and they have walls of books, pamphlets, advice, and guidance that almost nobody (except them) ever reads, and they've got brilliant strategies, too. But they know they lack the time, money, and community support they need to fully execute them.

I'm tired of seeing so many people giving of themselves to support others, then seeing their frustration and despair as they continually come up short. Instead of complaining, I'm going to attempt to offer and explain what might be a simple solution to a complex problem. You can be the judge.

Unless you're a drug dealer, my proposed solution shouldn't be a threat to anyone's authority, safety, or job security. In fact, I think it will enhance it. Again, I'll let you be the judge.

Before I present a possible solution, let me further define the scope of the problem and the obstacles currently making things difficult for those trying to help solve it. Then I'll share my ideas for overcoming those obstacles.

In no particular order:

1. Getting parents to listen is a challenge. Far too many think it's "not their kid" using drugs, until they find out the hard way that it is. I've attended far too many heavily promoted, drug awareness meetings hosted at high schools and event centers that almost nobody bothered to show up for. Here's something I'd like you to think about: What if there was a way to reach and help large numbers of parents,

hundreds or thousands of them at a time, easily and often, without expense? What if there was a way for parents to find out first, rather than last, that their kids were experimenting with drugs, or better yet, keep them from experimenting with drugs in the first place?

2. Getting some school administrators to acknowledge the severity of their local substance abuse problem can be a challenge. Getting them to do something about it, once they do, can be an even bigger challenge. Nobody wants the stigma and bad press associated with having drug problems in their schools. Administrators have to answer to their school board and to their community. They've typically got lots of other problems and sometimes, in the short term, it can seem easier to pretend there isn't a drug issue and sweep it under the rug—or update their résumé and go somewhere else—than admit there is a drug problem and do something about it. But what if there was a way for school and community leaders to turn negative press into positive press and demonstrate proactive leadership instead of having to backpedal reactively from a crisis? What if it could be done in a way that would turn parents into allies and a base of broader support instead of vocal opponents publicly leveling criticism? I'll get to that.

3. There is often a lack of cooperation, coordinated effort, and agreed-upon goals among people and organizations who are already working toward reducing drug use in local communities. Let me describe this in a different way. I'd like you to think about your favorite song. Maybe it was a top ten or maybe even a number one hit on the charts at one time. Now imagine what that exact same song, played by those exact same musicians, the exact same way, note by note, using the exact same instruments would sound like if each musician in the band decided to start playing his or her part at a different time, or chose not to play his or her part at all. It would sound like a mess; total noise, right? The difference between a total mess full of absolute noise and being a top ten or number one hit was just one thing: coordinated timing toward a common goal. What if there was a way for parents, schools, coalitions, politicians, law enforcement, treatment professionals, and anyone else who wanted to join in, to play their parts together, toward a common goal, without interfering with their other duties? How much more powerful would the whole effort be compared to the disorganized and random sum of the parts?

4. Funding. If you talk to community leaders or law enforcement agencies whose

special efforts or task forces are funded by grants, you will discover that many of them live in constant fear that their funding will dry up and that the momentum they've created will come to a grinding halt. Because funding usually lasts for a period of time, they worry about being able to meet their objectives before funding runs out. How much more motivated, disciplined, and committed do you think the people and organizations in those predicaments would be if they had no fear of their efforts being in vain or their funding getting pulled? How much more energized, committed, and dedicated do you think they would be if they had the tools and resources they needed and the time to finish the initiatives they started?

5. Time. Community leaders are busy. Their time and use of budgetary funds are subject to scrutiny. They aren't sitting around bored looking for something to do. Most don't have extra time to read a handful of books, pamphlets, and reports, attend additional meetings, or execute a bunch of grandiose ideas even if they did take the time to listen to them or had money in their budgets. What this means is that a solution requiring their participation should take less than a minute to explain, not affect their budget, and be able to be executed during the

course of their regular duties without adding to their work.

I recognize that the parents and community leaders most capable of implementing and executing a collaborative solution to the drug problem are busy people. Their plates are full and their resources are limited. That's why it's important to focus on low-cost and no-cost strategies that don't interfere with their regular responsibilities.

I'm going to ask you to suspend belief and forget what you know or think you know about drug prevention efforts in your household, town, state, and country. Let me be blunt. Let's talk about kids, parents, and community leaders. I'm an advocate for properly administered home drug testing programs and that's why my organization has donated and is continuing to donate hundreds of thousands of dollars' worth of free home drug test vouchers to proactive communities across the country, and we are willing to donate to support yours.

Legislators and law enforcement folks are working hard and risking their lives to reduce the supply of drugs. I wake up every day focused on ways to reduce the demand.

Let's Talk about Community Leaders (Police, School Districts, and Church Groups)

Let me tell you about a school district in a suburb of Milwaukee. Several years ago, I met a superintendent who was facing a vocal and angry mob of parents who were complaining because there were three drug-related arrests in a forty-five-day period in their local high school. The parents were pointing fingers, complaining that the school wasn't safe, and blaming the school leaders and local police for the problems.

He met with his board and they worked together to create a win-win scenario that transformed the angry parents into allies instead of adversaries. His message to the parents was simple: He told them they were right. The school wasn't as safe as it could be.

He explained that they were doing all they could with what they had to work with and it still wasn't enough. He asked for their help. He talked about home drug testing, gave them vouchers for free kits, and asked them to do their part to keep the drug problems from ever getting to school in the first place.

In another school district that originally received printed vouchers for free home drug test kits, the school leaders voiced a concern that they felt parents in their district were hesitant to ask for them face-to-face from a school employee. The school leaders wanted to know how to reach the parents of "Annie the A-Student" and "Johnny Football Hero" because in their close-knit community, they couldn't envision parents of those kids stopping by the office to request a voucher if they merely suspected a possible problem.

That's where the idea for creating an electronic version of the voucher came from. When parents realized they could get a free home drug test kit and keep their privacy in check, voucher redemption rates went up 500%.

The lesson learned was that there had to be a simple, private way for parents in need to get help without creating more problems and suspicion at school or with local law enforcement officials. Nothing could be easier for parents than going online and having a kit sent to their house without having to interact with another community member, school official, or police officer.

In one small rural town, with a population of 3,000, I saw with my own eyes what was possible when community leaders worked together: I saw what had to be 700 – 800 people get together at a middle school gymnasium for a drug awareness meeting. In a town of 3,000, where it's the norm for parents to assume that their kids would never use drugs, that was an amazing accomplishment.

How'd they do it? It was a total team effort. The city sent out messages on the utility bills. The schools sent messages to parents and announced the meeting at athletic events. Local businesses put up signs. The Chamber of Commerce mentioned it at meetings. The local radio stations and newspapers spread the word, too. It was awesome!

The lesson learned there was how easy it was for community leaders to get a single, congruent message to members of their community without much extra work or expense. And this is an important distinction and advantage.

Why? Because it's not like drug dealers can advertise their business on radio, television, or in the newspaper. Drug dealers have to work secretly, slowly, and carefully, one-on-one with their clients. That gives them a huge disadvantage compared to what community leaders working together can do. However, as Edmund Burke said, "All that is necessary for the triumph of evil is for good men to do nothing."

I've also noticed a shift in the way churches respond to these types of community challenges. In years past, I don't think it was uncommon for churches to build up walls around their congregations in an effort to shield and protect their members. However, as of late, I've seen more of them, including my own, becoming more outwardly focused and interested in reaching out to those in need of help.

Where I attend, church isn't viewed as a building or even a thing. It's what we do. It's being the answer to other people's prayers. Church is a verb.

Recently, we had a fabulous guest speaker at our church. I almost skipped that week but decided to go anyway, and I'm glad I did. As it turned out, the guest speaker was a former drug dealer. I can't fathom the idea of a former drug dealer coming into any church I ever attended as a kid, talking openly about the subject matter he was discussing.

Of course I couldn't resist, so I went up afterwards and asked for the opportunity to interview him for my work with the TestMyTeen.com project. Thankfully, he agreed.

As a precondition of the interview, I asked him to shoot straight and not sugarcoat anything. He made fun of just about every popular drug prevention effort. He called them boring and irrelevant and explained why some even helped him sell more drugs.

He talked about the naive parents of the "good kids" who thought they had nothing to worry about, when in fact those same kids were his best prospects. He shed light on how he bamboozled all his friends' parents who thought he was one of the "good kids," too, because he was an honor roll student, captain of the football team, and always used good manners. Little did the local parents know that he had been selling drugs in school since ninth grade and was making thousands of dollars a week from their kids, right under their noses.

In the course of the interview I learned how to discourage, frustrate, and demoralize a drug dealer. I simply asked him his thoughts about this hypothetical situation: I asked him, "What would you do if you wanted to set up shop and start selling drugs in a particular community and when you got there to check it out you found out that things were done differently than anything you'd seen before?" To be more specific, I asked him to imagine the following:

1. School, police, and community leaders all working together to make it possible for every household that wanted one to get a free home drug test kit, simply by going to a website and ordering one, privately and confidentially, with no record of the request.

2. Everywhere you see bumper stickers on police cars and school buses, and banners in gymnasiums telling parents how to be proactive and get free drug test kits and reward their teens for drug-free results.

3. At high school football or basketball games, thousands of potential customers' parents are being told over the loudspeaker about how easy it is to make sure their kids have a socially acceptable reason to say no to drugs.

4. Every year at middle school, junior high, and high school parent orientations, the

new batch of potential drug users are being reduced, if not cut out altogether, because parents are being told about the free kits and simple prevention strategies they could implement at home by themselves.

5. Implementation is occurring at the family level, using the same strategies that make drug-free workplaces safer. Imagine at playgrounds, locker rooms, bus stops, and dare I say parties, kids are saying, "No thanks. My parents test me."

Want to take a guess what he said next? He shook his head, smiled, and said he wouldn't want to do business there. He said he would go somewhere else. Why? It was because the rewards wouldn't be worth the risk!

But what if every community embraced this approach and put drug dealers on their heels, poisoned their wells, ruined their territories, and discouraged potential dealers from ever getting into the trade?

When kids are saying "No thanks, my parents test me," instead of "yes," demand for drugs goes down while the risk of drug dealers getting caught by angry parents as well as police officers skyrockets. It's bad for business.

Are there obstacles in achieving this vision? Of course.

Why am I so optimistic that it's possible to achieve this vision in spite of those obstacles?

1. The price is right. After registering at TestMyTeen.com, there's no cost to the community to distribute free home drug test vouchers donated by TestMyTeen.com. This means there is never a budget item to justify or renew. (Note that TestMyTeen.com will provide vouchers for free home drug tests as long as parents pay for shipping and handling. And to prevent abuse, there is a limit of one free kit per family.)

2. Online ordering and distribution systems have been set up to help communities execute and families administer their home drug testing programs. Videos have been created to explain how everything works so community leaders don't have to explain, inventory product, or manage anything. They just tell people who need the kits where to get them, which is usually their website.

3. Community leaders can simply promote their own websites doing the same stuff they already do, so there's no extra work. Police drive their cars anyway. Schools send their buses out on the roads anyway. Why not have bumper stickers on them that direct parents to resources on their sites? Parents go to school athletic events

anyway. Rosters and programs get printed anyway. Announcements get made during halftime of big games anyway. Drug dealers can't do any of that!

4. Random drug testing programs have made the American workplace safer, and you can't tell me that employers care more about their employees than parents care about their kids.

5. If almost everyone knows that you dial 9 1 1 in case of emergency, then why can't they be taught to go to the local police website and/or school website to get access to a free home drug test voucher?

6. When things work like they are supposed to:

   a. Kids will have socially acceptable excuses that make them safer.

   b. Parents will have peace of mind they deserve.

   c. School leaders can spend more time educating kids instead of dealing with a bunch of drug-related nonsense that parents could be preventing or nipping at the bud before it ever gets to school.

   d. Fewer police officers' lives will be put at risk.

Everybody (except the drug dealers) wins.

Here's the deal, now that you know what the plan is:

1. Your local police department, school district, and parent coalitions can get immediate access to a minimum of $5,000 worth of free home drug test kit vouchers simply by registering an account for free at http://www.testmyteen.com.

2. Your school, community, and law enforcement leaders now have the ability to get the word out to parents who need it without spending a bunch of money or time, and can pretty much execute this program while you're doing your normal duties.

3. You as a parent can inspect what you expect (a drug-free household) and share this concept with parents and community leaders in surrounding communities.

About the Authors

Mason Duchatschek

Mason Duchatschek is a co-founder of TestMyTeen.com, a #1 Amazon.com best-selling author and keynote speaker. He has spoken to thousands of teachers, school administrators, school resource officers, school board members, police chiefs, detectives, parents, counselors, teens, and even a few drug dealers, about drugs, peer pressure, addiction, and the culture that surrounds it. His drug prevention ideas have been featured on CNBC, Fox News, and CNN. Stories about his strategies have appeared in the New York Times, Newsweek, the Atlanta Journal Constitution, the Milwaukee Journal-Sentinel, and the St. Louis Post-Dispatch. He has also been a frequent guest on radio programs across the United States and Canada.

Sean Mulroney

As a teenager, Sean Mulroney was addicted to drugs and alcohol. He was first exposed to them at the age of six, and by the time he was thirteen years old, he was involved heavily in both drugs and alcohol. He watched many of his friends die young from drinking and driving, drug overdoses, and suicide. It took many years and the help of trusted adults for him to overcome his addictions.

He is the president and founder of the nonprofit organization Teens of America. Teens of America was created to educate America's youth on the dangers of bullying, drug and alcohol abuse, peer pressure, and suicide. Along with his co-host, John Martin, he has a radio show called Reality Check Nation. The show averages over 40,000 listeners and reaches audiences in thirty-five states. His show has recently expanded to reach new audiences in Ireland, France, Israel, England, and Canada. He has reached hundreds of thousands of parents and students via his website and multimedia assemblies as well.

Tina Meier

Tina Meier is the founder of the Megan Meier Foundation, a 501(c)(3) not-for-profit organization based in St. Charles, Missouri. She is a keynote speaker and internationally recognized expert on bullying, cyberbullying, internet safety, conflict resolution, the roles of parents and educators, sexting, and suicide awareness and prevention.

Through her organization, she and her staff have reached over 172,000 students, parents, and educators in 193 communities and thirty-two states.

She worked closely with Senator Scott Rupp and Governor Matt Blunt's Internet Task Force for the state of Missouri to help pass Senate Bill 818, which went into law on August 28, 2008. This law amended the harassment and stalking laws to include electronic communication.

Tina has continued to spread the Foundation's message and her daughter Megan's story through national and international media appearances such as network television stations, radio, news magazines, and syndicated talk shows. She also accepted a presidential invitation to attend the 2011 White House Anti-Bullying Conference, presented at the U.S. Department of Education's Safe and Drug-Free Schools National Conference in Washington, D.C., and served as a consultant during the production of the ABC Family movie Cyberbully.

Tina Meier resides in St. Louis, Missouri, with her daughter Allison.